ARGENTINA

R.L. Van

abdobooks.com

Published by Abdo Publishing, a division of ABDO, PO Box 398166, Minneapolis, Minnesota 55439. Copyright © 2023 by Abdo Consulting Group, Inc. International copyrights reserved in all countries. No part of this book may be reproduced in any form without written permission from the publisher. Big Buddy Books™ is a trademark and logo of Abdo Publishing.

Printed in the United States of America, North Mankato, Minnesota
102022
012023

Design: Emily O'Malley, Mighty Media, Inc.
Production: Mighty Media, Inc.
Editor: Jessica Rusick
Cover Photograph: Oomka/Shutterstock Images
Interior Photographs: A.RICARDO/Shutterstock Images, p. 23; Adrian Murphy/Shutterstock Images, p. 15; AM113/Shutterstock Images, pp. 21, 29 (top right); Andrey_Kuzmi/Shutterstock Images, p. 28 (bottom); buteo/Shutterstock Images, p. 6 (bottom); Diego Grandi/Shutterstock Images, p. 6 (top); fifg/Shutterstock Images, p. 29 (bottom); Frederic Legrand - COMEO/Shutterstock Images, p. 11; grebeshkovmaxim/Shutterstock Images, p. 7 (map); Guillermo Spelucin R/Shutterstock Images, p. 19; Ionov Vitaly/Shutterstock Images, p. 26 (left); Ivo Antonie de Rooij/Shutterstock Images, p. 26 (right); Julinzy/Shutterstock Images, p. 30 (flag); karlagarciav/iStockphoto, p. 27 (bottom); lukulo/iStockphoto, pp. 5 (compass), 7 (compass); Mariano Gaspar/Shutterstock Images, p. 27 (top right); Pav-Pro Photography Ltd/Shutterstock Images, p. 17; pawopa3336/iStockphoto, p. 25; Pyty/Shutterstock Images, p. 5 (map); railway fx/Shutterstock Images, p. 13; Roadsidephotographer/Shutterstock Images, p. 30 (currency); saiko3p/Shutterstock Images, p. 6 (middle); Sergey Rusakov/Shutterstock Images, p. 9; sunsinger/Shutterstock Images, p. 27 (top left); Wikimedia Commons, pp. 28 (top), 29 (top left)
Design Elements: Mighty Media, Inc.
Country population and area figures taken from the CIA World Factbook

Library of Congress Control Number: 2022940501

Publisher's Cataloging-in-Publication Data
Names: Van, R.L., author.
Title: Argentina / by R.L. Van
Description: Minneapolis, Minnesota : Abdo Publishing, 2023 | Series: Countries | Includes online resources and index.
Identifiers: ISBN 9781532199530 (lib. bdg.) | ISBN 9781098274733 (ebook)
Subjects: LCSH: Argentina--Juvenile literature. | South America--Juvenile literature. | Argentina--History--Juvenile literature. | Geography--Juvenile literature.
Classification: DDC 982--dc23

CONTENTS

Passport to Argentina 4
Important Cities 6
Argentina in History 8
An Important Symbol 12
Across the Land 14
Earning a Living 16
Life in Argentina 18
Famous Faces 20
A Great Country 24
Tour Book 26
Timeline 28
Argentina Up Close 30
Glossary 31
Online Resources 31
Index 32

PASSPORT TO ARGENTINA

Argentina is a country in southern South America. It borders five other countries and an ocean. It is the eighth-largest country in the world. More than 45 million people live there.

2

IMPORTANT CITIES

Buenos Aires is Argentina's **capital** and largest city. It is also the country's main port.

Córdoba is Argentina's second-largest city. Cars, tractors, cloth, and glass are made there.

Rosario is the country's third-largest city. It **exports** agricultural products, beef, and lumber.

ARGENTINA IN HISTORY

Native peoples were the first to live in what is now Argentina. They hunted, fished, and farmed. Europeans arrived in the 1500s. In 1580, the Spanish made a lasting settlement at Buenos Aires. Over time, they ruled the area.

The Quilmes Ruins were home to native peoples more than 1,000 years ago.

In 1816, Argentina declared independence from Spain. By the 1880s, the country had **united**. By the 1920s, meat and grain **exports** had made Argentina one of the world's richest countries. Starting in 1930, Argentina was led off and on by military leaders. The country struggled. Today, it is led by a president.

In October 2019, Alberto Fernández became Argentina's president.

AN IMPORTANT SYMBOL

Argentina's flag is blue and white. It has a sun in the center. The sun stands for freedom from Spain.

Argentina is a **federal republic**. The Senate and Chamber of Deputies make laws. The president is the head of state and government.

The blue on Argentina's flag represents the sky. The white represents snow in the Andes Mountains.

5

ACROSS THE LAND

Argentina has many types of land and wildlife. The Andes Mountains are in the west. The Pampas are grasslands in the country's center. Argentina also has penguins, capybaras, and fruit trees.

SAY IT

Pampas
PAM-puhs

Capybaras are the world's largest rodents.

EARNING A LIVING

In Argentina, most people have service jobs. Many help visitors to the country. Others work in factories. Farmers grow corn, soybeans, wheat, and fruit. They also produce beef. Shrimp, scallops, and squid come from Argentina's waters.

Grapes are one of Argentina's main crops.

7

LIFE IN ARGENTINA

Most of Argentina's people live in cities. Others live in the countryside. The people of Argentina enjoy eating beef. They drink maté tea and wine.

Soccer is Argentina's most popular sport. Car and horse racing are popular as well.

SAY IT

maté
MAH-teh

Desserts in Argentina often include dulce de leche, a milky caramel.

FAMOUS FACES

Pope Francis was born in Buenos Aires. His given name is Jorge Mario Bergoglio. Pope Francis was chosen as pope in 2013. He was the first pope from Latin America. As pope, he leads the Roman **Catholic** Church. Most of Argentina's people are Catholic.

Pope Francis is known for helping the poor.

Professional soccer player Lionel Messi was born in Rosario. His family moved to Spain when he was 13. Messi has played for Barcelona and Paris Saint-Germain. He also plays for Argentina's national team.

DID YOU KNOW?

In 2014, Lionel Messi led Argentina's national soccer team to the World Cup final.

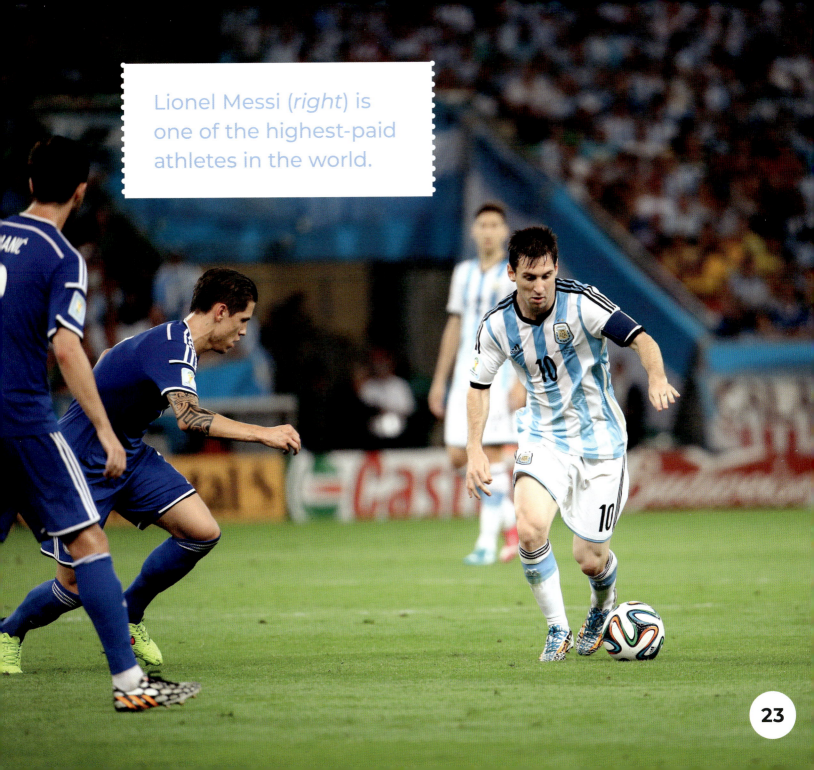
Lionel Messi (*right*) is one of the highest-paid athletes in the world.

A GREAT COUNTRY

Argentina is a land of beautiful waterfalls and mountains. The people and places that make up Argentina help make the world a more interesting place.

Mount Aconcagua in Argentina is the highest mountain in the Andes.

TOUR BOOK

If you ever visit Argentina, here are some places to go and things to do!

EXPLORE

Visit Ushuaia, one of the southernmost cities in the world. People travel there to ski, see whales and penguins, and get close to Antarctica.

SEE

Go to Iguazú Falls National Park. The enormous waterfalls reach as high as 269 feet (82 m)!

PLAY

Soccer is a big part of Argentina's culture. Play a game of soccer or watch a professional game!

EAT

Try dulce de leche. Or eat beef cooked over an open fire!

DO

In Argentina, gauchos are similar to cowboys. Visit an *estancia*, or ranch, to experience gaucho culture.

TIMELINE

1853
Argentina adopted a **constitution**.

1944
Author Jorge Luis Borges of Buenos Aires printed *Ficciones*. It was one of his most famous works.

1903
Buenos Aires police started solving crimes using the first workable system of identifying fingerprints. This system was developed by Argentinean Juan Vucetich.

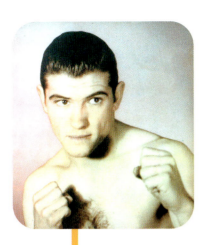

1954
Pascual Perez became the country's first World Boxing Champion.

2013
Cardinal Jorge Mario Bergoglio of Argentina was chosen as pope. He took the name Pope Francis.

1986
Star player Diego Maradona led the country's soccer team to win the World Cup.

ARGENTINA
UP CLOSE

Official Name
República Argentina
(Argentine Republic)

Flag

Population
46,245,668 (2022 est.)
32nd-most-populated country

Total Area
1,073,518 square miles
(2,780,400 sq km)
8th-largest country

Official Language
Spanish

Capital
Buenos Aires

Currency
Argentine peso

Form of Government
Federal republic

National Anthem
"Himno Nacional Argentino"
("Argentine National Anthem")

GLOSSARY

capital—a city where government leaders meet.

Catholic—of or relating to the Roman Catholic Church. This kind of Christianity has been around since the first century and is led by the pope.

constitution—the basic laws that govern a country or a state.

export—to send goods to another country for sale; these goods are called exports.

federal republic—a form of government in which the people choose the leader. The central government and the individual states share power.

unite—to come together for a purpose or action.

ONLINE RESOURCES

To learn more about Argentina, please visit **abdobooklinks.com** or scan this QR code. These links are routinely monitored and updated to provide the most current information available.

INDEX

Andes Mountains, 13, 14, 25
animals, 14, 15, 26

Borges, Jorge Luis, 28
Buenos Aires, 6, 7, 8, 20, 28, 30
businesses, 6, 16

Córdoba, 6, 7

Europe, 8, 10, 22

Fernández, Alberto, 11
flag, 12, 13, 30
food, 16, 17, 18, 19, 27
Francis (pope), 20, 21, 29

gauchos, 27
government, 10, 11, 12, 28, 30

Iguazú Falls, 26

language, 7, 30

Maradona, Diego, 29
Messi, Lionel, 22, 23
Mount Aconcagua, 25

Pampas, 14
Perez, Pascual, 29
plants, 14, 16, 17
population, 4, 7, 30

Quilmes Ruins, 9

religion, 20
Rosario, 6, 7, 22

size, 30
South America, 4
Spain, 8, 10, 12, 22
sports, 18, 22, 23, 27, 29

Ushuaia, 26

Vucetich, Juan, 28